V is for Vintage

A is for Airplane

B is for Bike

C is for Car

D is for Drive-in Movie

E is for Eggs

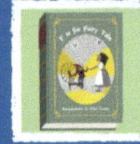
F is for Fairy Tale

G is for Gumball Machine

H is for Hot Air Balloon

I is for Ice Cream Truck

J is for Jukebox

K is for Kite

L is for Lava Lamp

M is for Milkman

N is for Needlework

O is for Operator

P is for Postcard

Q is for Quilt

R is for Roller Skates

S is for Sewing Machine

T is for Telephone

U is for Umbrella

V is for Vinyl

W is for Wagon

X is for Xmas

Y is for Yarn

Z is for Zoo

V is for Vintage

A is for Airplane

B is for Bike

C is for Car

D is for Drive-in Movie

E is for Eggs

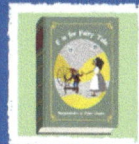

F is for Fairy Tale

G is for Gumball Machine

H is for Hot Air Balloon

I is for Ice Cream Truck

J is for Jukebox

K is for Kite

L is for Lava Lamp

M is for Milkman

N is for Needlework

O is for Operator

P is for Postcard

Q is for Quilt

R is for Roller Skates

S is for Sewing Machine

T is for Telephone

U is for Umbrella

V is for Vinyl

W is for Wagon

X is for Xmas

Y is for Yarn

Z is for Zoo

For my Father, Ballard Dean McPherson.

www.theenglishschoolhouse.com

Text copyright 2020 by Dr. Tamara Pizzoli
Pictures copyright 2020 by Adam Cox
All rights reserved.

ISBN: 978-0-9992108-5-7

V Is For Vintage

By Dr. Tamara Pizzoli

◇

ILLUSTRATED BY ADAM COX

A IS FOR AIRPLANE

B is for bicycle

C IS FOR CAR

VINTAGE 21

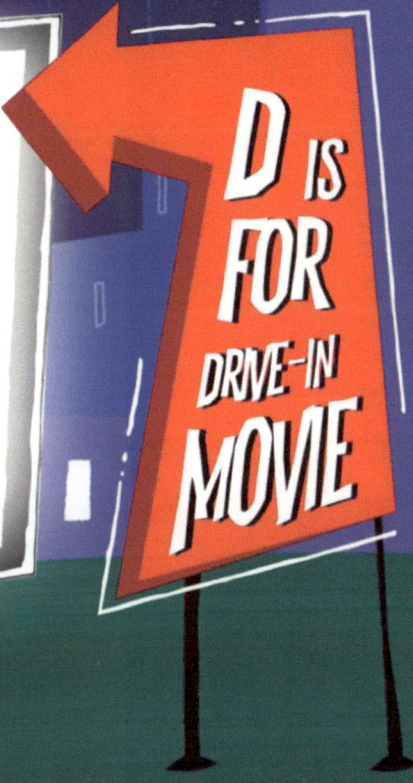

D IS FOR DRIVE-IN MOVIE

FARM FRESH

Eggs 25¢

E is for eggs

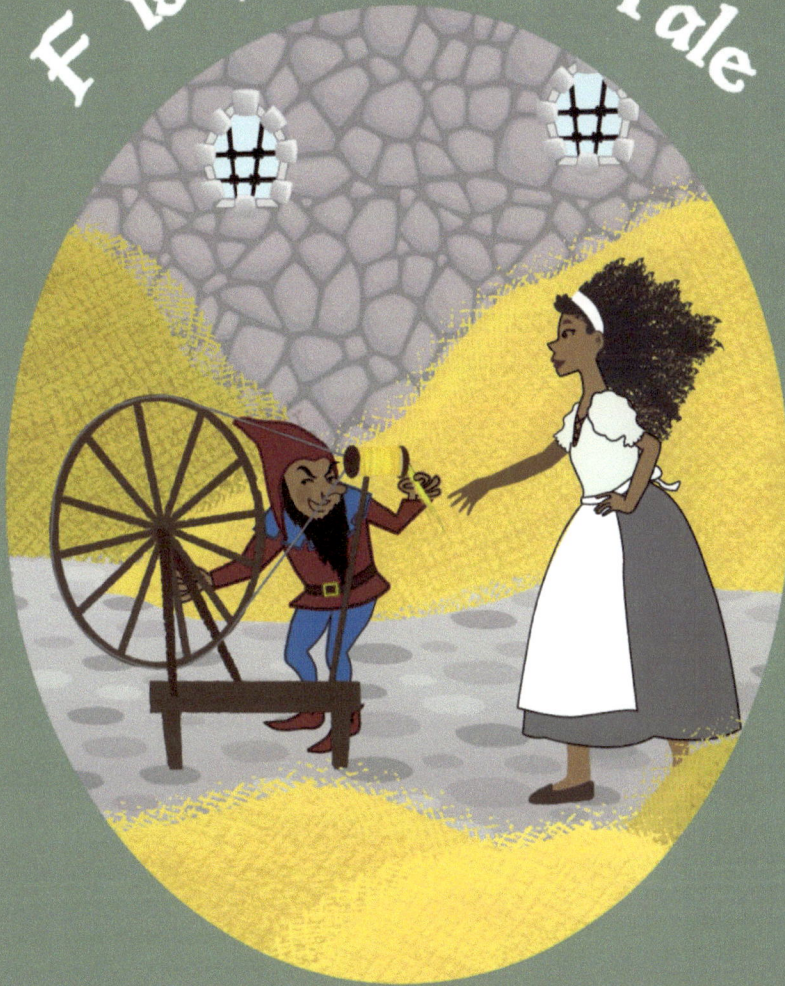

F is for Fairy Tale

Rumpelstiltskin & Other Classics

G is for
Gumball Machine

H is for
Hot Air Balloon

ICE CREAM

I is for
ice cream truck

J IS FOR JUKEBOX

K is for kite

L IS FOR
LAVA LAMP

M is for Milkman

CAIRO
the great pyramids

Ciao from
ROME

BIG THINGS HAPPEN HERE
IN
DALLAS
TEXAS

Postcard

P is for
POSTCARD

LONDON
AIR MAIL

THE ENGLISH SCHOOLHOUSE
147 LITERATURE LANE
BOOK LOVERSVILLE

POSTAGE STAMP

Q IS FOR QUILT

R is for Roller Skates

S is for sewing machine

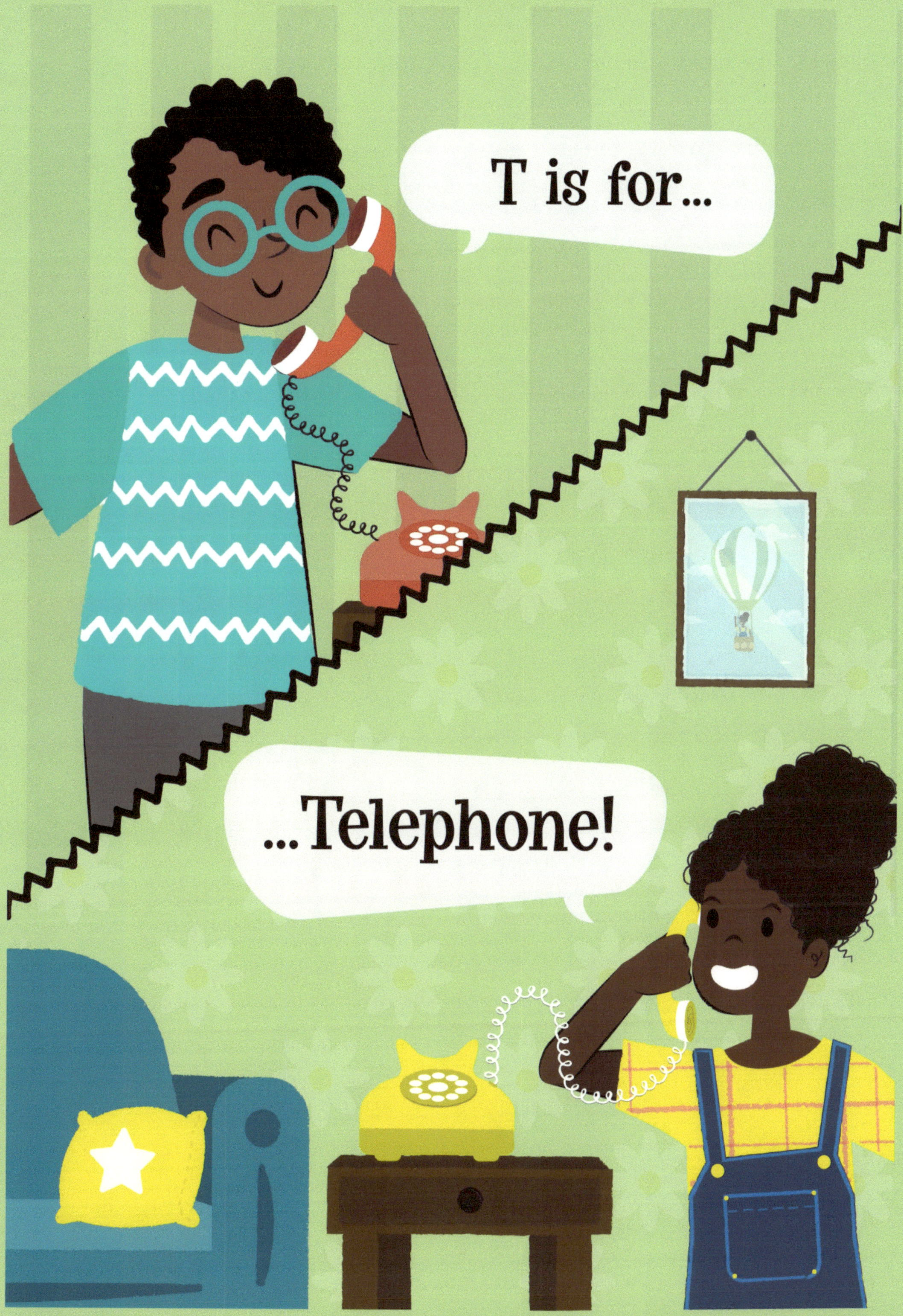
T is for...
...Telephone!

U is for Umbrella

V IS FOR VINYL

W IS FOR WAGON

X IS FOR XMAS

Y is for Yarn

Z is for

zoo

A note from the Author

Some of my earliest and fondest childhood memories include riding around with my father in Texas and stopping at antique shops that we'd happen upon along the way. My mother would groan and lament that we didn't need any more old stuff piling up in the house. If my father heard her complaints, he didn't show it.

He'd hop out the car and spend all the time he deemed necessary doing more browsing than buying. He rarely left an antique shop empty-handed. I remember riding in the backseat of his car and finding a rotation of what-nots that my mom called junk, but my father absolutely regarded as rare finds—dolls, rolodexes, telephones, and more. Some were broken and others weren't.

This book is a nod to the love of vintage that my father passed on to me. I still find rummaging through antique stores, searching for treasures, to be one of life's very best pastimes. My father's name is Ballard. He'd be happy you've picked up this book.

Enjoy,

Dr. Tamara Pizzoli

V is for Vintage

Encore

V is for Vintage

A is for Airplane

B is for Bike

C is for Car

D is for Drive-in Movie

E is for Eggs

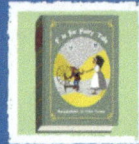
F is for Fairy Tale

G is for Gumball Machine

H is for Hot Air Balloon

I is for Ice Cream Truck

J is for Jukebox

K is for Kite

L is for Lava Lamp

M is for Milkman

N is for Needlework

O is for Operator

P is for Postcard

Q is for Quilt

R is for Roller Skates

S is for Sewing Machine

T is for Telephone

U is for Umbrella

V is for Vinyl

W is for Wagon

X is for Xmas

Y is for Yarn

Z is for Zoo

V IS FOR VINTAGE

**A is for
Airplane**

**B is for
Bike**

**C is for
Car**

**D is for
Drive-in Movie**

**E is for
Eggs**

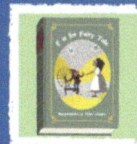
**F is for
Fairy Tale**

**G is for
Gumball Machine**

**H is for
Hot Air Balloon**

**I is for
Ice Cream Truck**

**J is for
Jukebox**

**K is for
Kite**

**L is for
Lava Lamp**

**M is for
Milkman**

**N is for
Needlework**

**O is for
Operator**

**P is for
Postcard**

**Q is for
Quilt**

**R is for
Roller Skates**

**S is for
Sewing Machine**

**T is for
Telephone**

**U is for
Umbrella**

**V is for
Vinyl**

**W is for
Wagon**

**X is for
Xmas**

**Y is for
Yarn**

**Z is for
Zoo**

www.ingramcontent.com/pod-product-compliance
Lightning Source LLC
Chambersburg PA
CBHW060825090426

42738CB00003B/105